Sunday
Prayers

Our Father . . .

Our Father, who art in heaven,
hallowed be thy name.
Thy kingdom come.
Thy will be done on earth,
as it is in heaven.
Give us this day our daily bread.
And forgive us our trespasses,
as we forgive those
who trespass against us.
And lead us not into temptation,
but deliver us from evil.
Amen.

Thank you for this day . . .

O Almighty God,
we thank you for this special day
which you have given us
for worship and rest.
Help us to keep it holy,
as the best day in all the week.
Teach everyone to love and honor
your day, that we may all rejoice
and be glad in it.

For this new Sunday
with its light,
For rest and shelter
of the night,
I thank you, heavenly Father.
Through this new week
but just begun,
Be near, and help us
every one
To please you, heavenly Father.

How great is God . . .

All things bright and beautiful,
all creatures great and small,
all things wise and wonderful,
the Lord God made them all.

He gave us eyes to see them,
and lips that we might tell,
how great is God Almighty,
who has made all things well.

Thank you, God . . .

Thank you for each happy day,
For fun, for friends,
  and work and play;
Thank you for your loving care,
Here at home and everywhere.

Loving Father, we thank you
for the wonderful things
which you have given to us:
For the beautiful sun,
For the rain
  which makes things grow,
For the woods and the fields,
For the sea and the sky,
For the flowers and the birds,
and for all your gifts to us.

Everything around us rejoices;
Make us also to rejoice:
  and give us thankful hearts.

Forgive me, God . . .

Our Father in heaven:
Please forgive me for the things
I have done wrong:
For bad temper and angry words;
For being greedy
  and wanting the best for myself;
For making other people unhappy:
Forgive me, heavenly Father.

Please, God . . .

Please God, look after all those
who stay behind at home
when others go out to school,
or work or play.
   Bless the ones who are too young
or too old to go,
and those who look after them.
   Bless those who get things
ready for us when we get home,
and help us to say thank you
to them.
   We pray especially for those
who stay at home because they
are ill.

Dear Father of the world family, please take care of all children everywhere. Keep them safe from danger, and help them grow up strong and good.

Help me, God . . .

O Lord, open my eyes,
  to see what is beautiful;
My mind, to know what is true:
My heart, to love what is good:
For Jesus' sake.

Lord Jesus, take me this day
and use me. Take my lips
and speak through them.
Take my mind and think through it.
Take my will and act through it,
and fill my heart with love for you.

MY OWN
SUNDAY PRAYERS

Everyday Prayers

Sunday

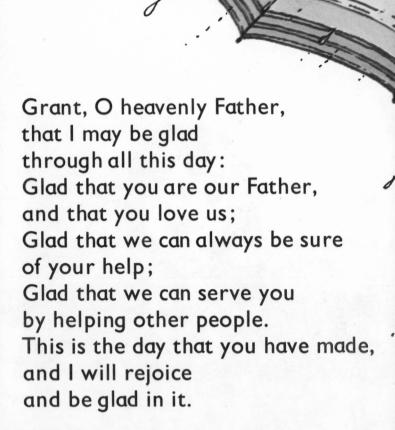

Grant, O heavenly Father,
that I may be glad
through all this day:
Glad that you are our Father,
and that you love us;
Glad that we can always be sure
of your help;
Glad that we can serve you
by helping other people.
This is the day that you have made,
and I will rejoice
and be glad in it.

Monday

Father, thank you for the night,
And for the pleasant morning light;
For rest and food and loving care,
And all that makes the day so fair.
Help me to do the things I should,
To be to others kind and good;
In all I do at work or play
To grow more loving every day.

Tuesday

Jesus, may I be like you;
Loving, kind in all I do;
Kind and happy when I play
Close beside you all the day.

Heavenly Father,
you have given this new day to me.
Help me to make it one
that pleases you by doing my best
in everything, because I love you.

Wednesday

Thank you, God, for this new day
In my school to work and play.
Please be with me all day long,
In every story, game and song.
May all the happy things we do
Make you, our Father, happy too.

Thursday

Thank you, Lord Jesus,
that you love us the same today
as yesterday.

Lord Jesus, I pray for those
who will be unhappy today:
for mothers who have no food
to cook for their children;
for fathers who cannot earn
enough money for their families;
for children who are sick
or frightened;
and for those who are alone
and without people to love them.

Friday

Thank you, God, for the day-time
when I can be awake and busy.
Thank you for all there is
for me to do today:
new things to find out,
friends and games to play with.
Thank you for the sun
that gives us warmth and light
to see by.

Saturday

For this new morning with its light,
    Father, I thank you.
For rest and shelter of the night,
    Father, I thank you;
For health and food,
    for love and friends
For everything your goodness sends,
    Father in heaven, I thank you.

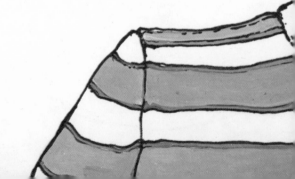

MY OWN
EVERYDAY PRAYERS

Goodnight Prayers

Sunday

Father, unto you we raise
Hearts and voices full of praise.
Bless us waking, guard us sleeping,
Through this night and all our days.

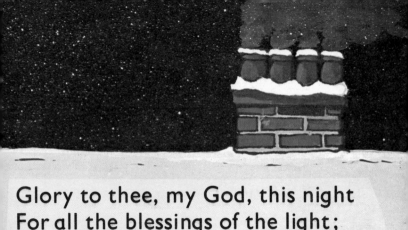

Glory to thee, my God, this night
For all the blessings of the light;
Keep me, O keep me, King of kings,
Beneath thy own almighty wings.

Tuesday

Jesus, tender Shepherd, hear me;
Bless your little lamb tonight;
Through the darkness
   please be near me;
Keep me safe till morning light.

All this day your hand has led me,
And I thank you for your care;
You have warmed and clothed
   and fed me;
Listen to my evening prayer.

Wednesday

O God, our heavenly Father,
bless and keep your children
all over the world,
this night and for ever.

Thursday

Jesus, friend of little children,
Be a friend to me;
Take my hand and ever keep me
Close to thee.

Friday

Loving Father, I'm sorry
for the wrong things that I have said
or thought or done today.
I'm sorry if I made others unhappy,
but most of all, help me
to be sorry if I have hurt you.

God the Father, bless us;
God the Son, defend us;
God the Spirit, keep us
Now and evermore.

Saturday

In our work and play God leads us,
Every step we take.
In our sleep he will be near us,
Watching till we wake.

MY OWN
GOODNIGHT PRAYERS

Everyday Graces

Sunday

Thank you for the world so sweet,
Thank you for the food we eat.
Thank you for the birds that sing,
Thank you, God, for everything.

Monday

All good gifts around us
Are sent from heaven above.
Then thank the Lord,
O thank the Lord
For all his love.

Tuesday

God is great, God is good,
Thank you, God, for all our food.

Wednesday

For every cup and plateful,
God make us truly grateful.

For health and strength
and daily food
we praise your name
O Lord.

Thursday

For food and drink and happy days,
Accept our gratitude and praise;
In serving others, Lord, we do
Express our thankfulness to you.

Friday

We thank you,
Father, for your care
For all your children everywhere.
As you feed us all our days
May our lives be filled with praise.

Saturday

Praise God,
from whom all blessings flow,
Praise him,
all creatures here below,
Praise him above,
you heavenly host,
Praise
Father, Son and Holy Ghost.

MY OWN
EVERYDAY GRACES